House Rules

All of the games in this book, although some of them may seem like games your buddy Timmy invented on his 19th birthday, were created on Irish soil.

You are hereby encouraged to take the games inside this finely crafted journal and let your imaginations run wild, change the rules and above all enjoy yourselves.

Now for the fine print:
Drink responsibly and don't be too much of a bowsy*.

Lastly, In the words of the great Billy Barry Murphy;

"Let's drink like cheap kings 'til we can't see."

First Published in 2010 by;
Billy Barry Publishing, Chicago, IL.

No vegetarians were harmed in the making of this book.

All picture credits go to the talented Lorenzo Bonilla. Design and layout by Jason Holland and Scott Hammond

ISBN: 978-0-615-40153-9

The Beef O' Keefe's Guide to

Irish
Drinking
Games

Memoirs of a Bowsy*

Beef O' Keefe

Billy Barry Publishing
Chicago

Don't open this book if you value your Liver!

Seriously!!

DON'T OPEN THIS BOOK.

You're one persistent Bollix* aren't ya!

Table of Contents

Inspiring Story

The Beef came home from the pub late one Friday evening stinking drunk, as he often did, and crept into bed beside his wife who was already asleep.

He gave her a peck on the cheek and fell asleep. When he awoke he found a strange man standing at the end of his bed wearing a long, flowing white robe. "Who the hell are you?" barked Beef, "and what are you doing in me bedroom?" The mysterious man answered "This isn't your bedroom and I'm St Peter."

Beef was stunned "You mean I'm dead!!! That can't be, I have so much to live for, I haven't even said goodbye to the family...ya have to send me back straight away."

St Peter replied "Yes my son you can be reincarnated but there is a catch. We can only send you back as a dog or a hen." Beef was devastated, but knowing there was a farm not far from his house, he asked to be sent back as a hen.

A flash of light later he was covered in feathers and clucking around pecking the ground for seed. "This ain't so bad" he thought until he felt this strange feeling welling up inside him.

The farmyard rooster strolled over and said,
"So you're the new hen, how are you enjoying your first day here?"

"It's not so bad" replies Beef, "but I have this strange feeling inside me like I'm about to explode."

"You're ovulating" explained the rooster, "don't tell me you've never laid an egg before?"

"Never" replies Beef.

"Well just relax and let it happen."

And so he did and after a few uncomfortable seconds later, an egg pops out from under his tail. An immense feeling of relief swept over him and his emotions got the better of him as he experienced motherhood for the first time.

When he laid his second egg, the feeling of happiness was overwhelming and he knew that being reincarnated as a hen was the best thing that ever happened to him...ever!!!

The joy kept coming and as he was just about to lay his third egg he felt a savage smack on the back of his head and heard his wife shouting "Beef, wake up you drunken bollox*, you're shitting the bed."

The Beef O' Keefe Hangover Ratings

1 star hangover ⭐

No pain. No real feeling of illness. You slept in your own bed and when you woke up there were no traffic cones or neighbors in there with you.

You are still able to function relatively well on the energy stored up from all those vodka and Red Bulls.

However, you can drink 10 bottles of water and still feel like you just licked a camel.

Even vegetarians are craving a cheeseburger and a bag of fries.

2 star hangover ⭐ ⭐

No pain, but there's definitely something missing. You may look okay but you have the attention span and mental capacity of a turnip.

The coffee you're hugging to try and stay focused is only fuelling your growling belly, which is craving a dirty fry*.

Although you have a nice playful demeanor about you, you are costing your employer valuable money because all you can really handle is some light filing, a heated online chat with a lemming or writing junk e-mails.

3 star hangover ★ ★ ★

You wake up in bed with your shoes and socks on.

Slight headache. Stomach feels polluted. You are definitely a space cadet, wishing you were outside chasing fairies.

Anytime a guy or girl walks by you gag because their perfume/aftershave reminds you of the random gin shots you chugged with your alcoholic friends after the bouncer kicked you out on your arse* at 1:45 am.

Life would be better right now if you were in your bed with a couple of cream doughnuts and a liter of coke watching daytime TV.

You've had 4 cups of coffee, a gallon of water, 2 Sausage Rolls and a liter of diet coke but you haven't peed once. Everyone knows who is farting though.

4 star hangover ★ ★ ★ ★

You have lost the will to live. Your head is throbbing and you can't speak too quickly or else you might spew.

Your boss has already turfed* you out of it for being late and has turned his nose up at the smell of shite* off you.

You wore nice clothes, but you smell of socks, and you can't hide the fact that you either shaved with a shovel or it looks like you put your make-up on while sitting on the washing machine.

Your teeth have their own individual sweaters. Your eyes look like one big vein and your hairstyle makes you look like a pervert.

You would give a weeks pay for one of the following – home time, a doughnut and somewhere to be alone or a good excuse to cry.

You scare small children in the street just by walking past them.

5 star hangover ★ ★ ★ ★ ★

You have a second heartbeat in your head, which is actually annoying the employee who sits next to you.

Vodka vapor is seeping out of every pore and making you dizzy.

You still have toothpaste crust in the corners of your mouth from brushing your teeth.

Your body has lost the ability to generate saliva and your tongue is suffocating you.

You'd cry but that would take the last drop of moisture left in your body.

Death seems pretty good right now.

Your boss doesn't even get mad at you and your co-workers think that your dog just died because you look so pathetic.

You should have called in sick because, let's face it, all you can manage to do is breathe.....very gently.

6 star hangover ★ ★ ★ ★ ★ ★

You arrive home and nose dive into bed.

The last thing that ran through your mind were the curry chips on the pillow beside you and the sausage behind your ear.

You get about 2 hours sleep until the noises inside your head wake you up.

You notice that your bed has been cleared for take-off and no matter what you do now, you're going to puke.

You stumble out of bed and find that the floor is sucking you into the hole in the middle of the room.

After walking along the skirting boards on alternating walls knocking off all the pictures, you find the toilet.

If you're lucky you'll remember to lift the lid before you explode and wake the whole house up with your drowning Buffalo impression.

You sit there on the floor in your woolly socks and y-fronts, hugging the only friend in the world you have left (the toilet), randomly continuing to make walrus noises, spitting and farting.

Tears stream down your face.

You are convinced that you are starting to turn yourself inside out and swear that you saw your pancreas shoot out of your mouth on the last wretch.

You have a vague recollection of calling your boss at 4am to sing your favorite karaoke song.

Work is simply not an option.

The whole day is spent trying to avoid anything that might make you sick again, like moving.

You vow never to touch a drop again and who knows for the next two or three hours at least you might even succeed.

OK, now hands up all those who have never had a six star hangover!!

Thought so!!

Chapter 1
Day Sessions

Defined as a group of at least 2 people drinking during the day and into the evening. As you can imagine, all you really need to get a good day session going is some drinking buddies, some drink, a day and an imagination.

However, day sessions are not for the faint hearted. Think of Saint Paddies Day, Super bowl Sunday or a bachelor/bachelorette weekend and then don't even consider thinking of the following day. Total dedication and commitment are needed.

The day session is a special occasion in any calendar. In younger years the day session is taken for granted as idle days are spent sipping back on Granpa's old cough medicine and taking the mick* out of your closest friends. In direct contrast to the day sessions in later years, which are more than often pre-planned excursions or are started by chance with a few recovery drinks the next morning.

The day session generally ends up with childish banter* involving wedgies and headlocks, with even the most refined of button nosed ladies and gentlemen finding it hard not to indulge in some harmless teenage banter.

For the day session a couple of slabs of beer are usually pre-required or a keg. But at least enough to get you started and last you through until a mid-day beer run.

Irish Open

Players: + **(teams of two)**
Buzz Type: High
Equipment: Golf course, golf clubs, beer.

The goal of this game is to have the lowest score for 18 holes of golf.

Your score is determined by totalling your teams best score on each hole and subtracting the combined number of beers the two of you drank throughout the round.

Paddy Dunne tried to screw the system by bringing the biggest pisshead* he could find and shooting a round of 82. Not on.

Irish Roulette

Players: 🎩 🎩 +
Buzz Type: **Medium** 🍺 🍺
Equipment: **CD Player with multiple CD loader and shuffle feature, CD's and beer.**

This is a game for any occasion.

Each player picks a CD with 10 or more songs on it.

Load a CD player with all of the CD's and press shuffle.

Every time a song from your CD is played you have to finish your beer or drink before the song ends.

If you don't finish you have to drink another beer during the next player's turn.

Usually only 3-5 people can play depending on the CD player's capacity.

Alternatively you can pick one album or compilation, divide out a few songs to each player, and play as above.

Another option is to select shuffle on your i-pod and make up rules as you go along.

The penalty for not finishing your drink is a shot of liquor or a good, solid kick up the arse*.

D.I.S.H.C.O.

Blackies Dice

Players: 🍀 🍀
Buzz Type: **Medium** 🍺 🍺
Equipment: **Rectangular table, 1 or 2 dice, tape, beer.**

Mark zones on each end of the table with the tape, about 4-5 inches from the edges. Get two teams of two, and sit at opposite ends with your partner, trying to roll the dice into the end zones.

If the dice land in your opponent's zone, you get that number of points and they have to drink that many fingers each.

If you roll doubles, both in the end zone, your opponents have to drink double what is showing on the dice. However, you only get as many points as are showing.

Play to 50 or whatever you feel like.

Add penalties for rolling dice off the table before they cross the end zone as you would like.

You can also place two extra lines in the middle of the table about three inches from the middle on each side. If you don't roll your dice past these lines, you drink double whatever is showing.

This is a great game for a tournament and the skill levels can be a major factor.

So don't pick the peg-legged* donkey on your team.

Shot Hunter

 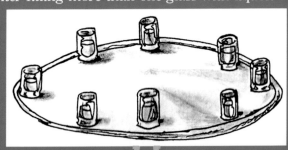
One Hunter is nominated to start the game.

All participants, except the hunter, have a shot glass in front of them.

The hunter, without letting any of the other players see, fills one glass with any clear liquor and the rest are filled with water. This filling of the glasses can be done on a tray, out of sight of the other players, and handed out.

The hunter then turns their back for 5-10 seconds while all the other players mix their glasses up. The key is for the hunter not to give the others enough time to check which glass is full of liquor.

The hunter then turns around and watches everyone take their shot, one by one, and has to guess which person had the liquor. The key is that all players must try and keep a straight face while drinking their shot.

If the hunter gets it right everyone at the table has to take a shot including the person who just had one. If the hunter guesses wrong, they must take a shot. This continues for each incorrect guess until the hunter guesses the right person.

The next person, or person who had taken the last shot, then becomes the hunter and the game goes on.

Skanks*; Hunter filling more than one glass with liquor.

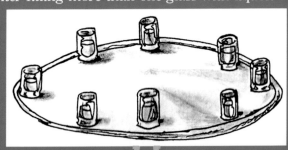

Shticks

Players: 👒👒+
Buzz Type: **Low** 🍺
Equipment: **Frisbee or tennis ball, two posts (cones, or anything that will stand a bottle), bottles of beer.**

Two posts are stuck in the ground a good distance apart from each other.

A beer bottle is placed on each post, and teams are divided up.

One team throws a Frisbee or a tennis ball at the other team's post/bottle.

If they hit the bottle off the post, and it hits the ground, the other team drinks a full beer. If the bottle is caught before it hits the ground, the throwing team drinks a full beer.

Players must keep their good arm behind their backs when catching.

If the frisbee or ball misses the post altogether, it must be caught, otherwise it's a drink.

If the Frisbee or ball doesn't make it to the post, it's a drink.

If the throw isn't catchable, it's a drink.

Forfeits – Eat Grass, lick the Frisbee, hold the post and run around it 20 times as fast as possible.

The Titanic

Players: 🎩🎩+
Buzz Type: High 🍺🍺🍺
Equipment: **Pint glass, small container (bottle cap etc), beer or liquor.**

Get a pint glass and fill it with as much beer as you like.

Float a small container in the beer.

You have to pour at least a drop of beer into the container, without sinking it. If you succeed, the person beside you tries and so on.

If you sink the cap you have to drink whatever is in the glass.

You can try dropping liquor into the container so the resulting gypsy potion will have some bite to it.

Try it with your bad hands!

Fact:

The Titanic was built in Belfast in 1912, "no wonder the bloody thing sank" some smart arse* said!

Cruisin'

Fire in the Hole

Players: +
Buzz Type: **Medium**
Equipment: **Pint glass (any container with wide opening), small coin, lit cigarette, beer, napkin or tissue.**

Fill the pint glass with as much beer as you want and cover the top with a napkin or tissue. Then place the coin in the center of the napkin.

Then, with a lit cigarette, burn holes into the napkin around the coin.

The person who makes the coin fall in, has to chug the beer including whatever ash and napkin debris fall in..

Try not to light the napkin on fire!

Start again.

Flamin' Drunk*

Bonus Section: 1
Beef's Favorite Irish Drinkin' Music

1   The Pogues

2   The Saw Doctors

3   The Dubliners

4   The Wolfe Tones

5   Christy Moore

6   Snow Patrol

7   Eire Lingus

8   Damien Dempsey

9   The Young Dubliners

10 The Kanyu Tree

Chapter 2
House Party

The house party is the arena for the classic drinking game party. If you can get the crowd involved, the house party can be the most rewarding and memorable occasion on the piss-head* calendar. The challenge is to get everyone on board from the get go by setting rules and initiating games as the night goes on. You'll always get a few moaners at every party that don't want to make the effort but the majority will win over even the most miserable of begrudging, self-righteous dry-shites*.

House party drinking games are chosen for their ability to cater to a bigger crowd of people and also their ability to engage the masses.

This chapter details games that can get a good mix of people involved. You can try and get one game flowing into the next or have several games running simultaneously (not recommended unless your mother agrees to organize the night for you).

The last couple of games in this chapter, that are a bit more brutal in nature, are intended for team bonding sessions or people who have already planned to spend the entire next day on the couch watching Baywatch or March of the Penguins.

House Party Set-up

Players: 🎩🎩🎩🎩🎩+
Buzz Factor: High 🍺🍺🍺
Equipment: Various.

A Random set of ideas that can be applied to any party setting:

1) 1 golf ball is in play. When it is dropped into someone's drink, the victim then has to chug the remains of their drink and carry on the game by dropping the golf ball into someone else's drink.

2) 100 Dollars in monopoly money can be given to each person on the way into the party. People have to win money through dares, truths, bets, stripping or any other method other than force to see who can amass the most money at the end of the night.

3) Every 30 minutes when the alarm sounds you have to swap a piece of clothing with the person you are talking to.

4) When a player leaves the table or goes to the toilet etc, they have to leave an item of clothing behind.

5) If you spill your drink, you remove an item of clothing PERMANENTLY.

6) Anyone who points during the night has to down their drink.

7) Nominate a Kingpin, i.e. the organizer or the person with the most buttons on their shirt. That person can call certain tasks throughout the night. When the Kingpin shouts "Snoz*" the last person to be touching noses with another person has to down a drink.

8) As soon as someone stands up, you can shout "Beer me ya bollox" at them to get you a new drink.

26

Suck 'em and See

Players: 🎩🎩🎩🎩+
Buzz Type: **High** 🍺🍺🍺
Equipment: **2 dice, glasses/cups, straws, beer.**

This is one of those great games where the object is to drink, not make the other team drink.

There are 2 teams of as many people as you want.

Each team has one six sided dice; each person has a straw and each team has 6 pints of beer.

The game starts with one person on each team frantically rolling the dice trying to get a one.

When he/she rolls a one, that team is allowed to drink the first cup.

However, the only way to drink is for all individual team members to suck the beer, through their straw, out of the same pint at the same time.

When the first cup is empty, the next person begins rolling for a two. When they get the two all members suck down the second cup.

This repeats with three, four, five, and six.

The object is to finish all six pints before the other team. The winners are of course expected to defend the honor.

You can use a coin for this game as well and try and flick heads every time.

Feckin Winker

Players: 🎩🎩🎩+
Buzz Type: Medium 🍺🍺
Equipment: Deck of cards, beer or liquor.

This game is best played with 6 people plus, sitting around a table.

Take a number of cards out of a deck that is equal to the number of people playing.

One of the cards has to be a king and one of the cards has to be an ace, the rest are number cards.

Dealer passes out a card to each person face down. Whoever gets dealt the ace is the pikey* and whoever gets the king is the cop. Once all of the cards have been passed out, everyone stares at everyone else around the table waiting to hear the words "the deal has been made". These words will be heard once the person who has the ace (the pikey) winks at someone around the table.

The person who has the king (the cop) is on alert to try to see who the pikey is. He/she wants to catch the pikey winking at someone.

Once someone has been winked at by the pikey and that person declares "the deal has been made" the cop reveals himself and tries to guess who the pikey is (the person who winked).

The cop then guesses one by one who he/she thinks the pikey is. Each time the cop guesses wrong, he/she has to take a drink. This goes on until the cop guesses who the pikey is.

It's great to watch the cop go through everyone around the table while having to slam beers for each incorrect guess. Also, if the pikey happens to wink at the cop, the pikey is automatically busted and has to drink a full beer.

Rule of thumb – Never trust a pikey!
...(see movie 'Snatch' for details)

Piss Your Beer Away

Players: +

Buzz Type: **Medium**

Equipment: **2 bottles, tape/chalk.**

This game is a perfect partner to Suck 'em and See.

Place two beer bottles on the ground (it is recommended doing this outside).

Draw a circle with an 18 inch radius around each bottle.

During a night of heavy drinking, have your team piss into the other teams bottle from outside the 18 inch radius. Whomever fills the other teams bottle first is the winner!

The loser gives the rest of their beer to the winners. So you had better have your pissin goggles on.

"I have never in all my years seen a lady take part in this one, but I'll marry her on the spot if I do."
Beef O' Keefe, 1999.

Windy Bollox

Players: ♣♣♣♣♣♣♣♣+
Buzz Type: High 🍺🍺🍺
Equipment: Large balloons, large bottles of beer or cider (preferably 40 OZ+).

This is a great game to get any party into the swing of things.

You need 2-3 teams with even numbers, alternating people in a line, girl, boy, girl...etc if possible.

Each team gets a large balloon and a large bottle of beer or cider.

When someone gives the signal, begin.

The first person on each team starts to drink. Each person drinks as much as they can without stopping and passes the bottle back along the line through their team.

As soon as the last person kills the bottle, the balloon is next.

The first person blows as much as they can until they are out of breath, passing it back along the line again.

The first team that pops the balloon, wins!

IMPORTANT NOTICE:
You can't pass the beer or the balloon back to the front. The last person or anchorman must be the one to finish. So if you're the last person and have some light-weights in your team, you'd better not be a windy bollox*.

After a few rounds the anchors on each team will be in bits!!

Roaring Numbers

Players: +

Buzz Type: **High**

Equipment: **Beer.**

The more the merrier for this absolute belter* of a game.

Sit in a circle.

Someone volunteers to go first and says 'one'.

Then, someone must take the initiative to say 'two', and so forth, progressing in a random order.

If two people speak at the same time, they both have to drink and the game starts again.

If no one says anything after about 2 seconds, the person who said the last number screams 'freeze'. That person then selects someone to take two drinks and the game starts again at one. (Anyone who is not trying usually gets nominated with these drinks.)

If someone talks at the same time as the person says 'freeze', they have to take three drinks.

Ten Minute Warning

Players: 👤+
Buzz Type: **Medium** 🍺🍺
Equipment: **Shot glass, beer.**

Every minute for ten minutes you take one shot of beer.

But here's the jimmy:

The first minute you take one shot of beer, the second minute you take two shots of beer, the third minute you take three shots of beer and so on.

It doesn't seem like it would be that hard but it has broken the best of men.

It does amount to a fair quantity, and it's a good challenge to put up to someone you know that thinks they're a bit of a legend.

Carpe Diem

Bonus Section: 2
Beef's Favorite Irish Clips on Youtube

1   Hardy Bucks

2   Savage Eye
    – Reasons why the Irish Drink.

3   Father Ted

4   Tommy Tiernan

5   Hector

6   Techno Viking
    – not quite Irish but we'll claim him.

7   Leprechaun in Mobile, Alabama.

8   The D'unbelievables

9   Killinaskully

10 Dave McSavage

Best Irish Drinkin' Movies

1   Intermission

2   Man about Dog

3   Waking Ned Devine

4   Michael Collins

5   The Butcher Boy

6   The Commitments

7   The Van

8   The Snapper

9   War of the Buttons

10 Into the West

11 ...and of course Braveheart
    (Up the Celts!!).

Chapter 3
Pre-game Sessions

The calm before the storm. Many a great night starts with a group of friends getting the juices flowing in anticipation of the main event to follow. This can be a great way to get the banter* going and to loosen the crew up before a big night.

You generally don't need a big group of people to get the pre-game going. Some of the best pre-games are spent among a couple of close friends sitting on a wall or at home relaxing.

The aim of the pre-game is to set the ball rolling and grease the pony* for the carnage to come.

Bladder Roulette

Players: 👒👒+
Buzz Type: High 🍺🍺🍺
Equipment: **6 shot glasses, bottle of clear liquor and a spinner.**

Firstly, you fill all the shot glasses with water and arrange them in a circle around a bottle or pen or any other thing you can spin.

First person spins the bottle and drinks the shot the spinner points to when it stops.

They then fill that glass with liquor.

If the next person were to land on that same glass they would drink the liquor, and refill it with water.

There is the potential for some people to be completely sober in this game but in reality, don't worry, everyone gets blocked*!

Chase The Ace

Players: ♣♣♣♣+
Buzz Type: High 🍺🍺🍺
Equipment: **2 dice and 2 cups to shuffle the dice, shot glass and liquor.**

This is a beautifully crafted game that comprises speed, fear and simplicity.

Everyone sits around a table.

Two people sitting opposite each other get a cup and a die.

They roll until they get a one.

When you get a one, you pass the cup and die clockwise to the next player.

Each player rolls the die until they get a one.

If you end up with both cups, you have to drink the shot.

You can also play this by flicking a coin to land on heads.

Priceless!

Tractor Pull

Players: 👒+

Buzz Type: **Deadly** 🍺🍺🍺🍺

Equipment: **6 cups and a shot glass per person playing, beer, stopwatch.**

You will need an official timekeeper to keep track of the competitors times.

The more serious the competition the better.

Line up each cup on a table and put one shot of beer in the first one, two in the second, three in the third, four in the fourth, five in the fifth and six shots in the sixth.

The first player holds the first cup (the cup with one shot of beer) in his hand.

The timekeeper is ready with the stopwatch and begins timing when the cup hits the players mouth.

The players goal is to finish all of the cups in one minute.

The finish time is key, however, if the gladiator doesn't finish all the cups his results are based on the amount of beer he has finished.

It is very important that the players start with the cup containing one shot, otherwise the game is very easy to complete.

The village record on this challenge was 21.8 seconds, held by the famous Titzy Dooley.

Last Man Standing

Players: 🎩🎩🎩+
Buzz Type: **Medium** 🍺🍺
Equipment: **Pack of cards, beer or liquor.**

Firstly you take out a set of four matching cards for each player i.e. if there are 4 players you take 4 aces, 4 kings, 4 queens and 4 jacks out of the pack.

The rest of the pack is then put away, until another player wants to join in.

The cards are then shuffled and 4 cards are dealt to each player.

When the dealer shouts go, each player places one card on the table to their left and then picks up the card the player to his right has left down.

Players keep passing and picking cards like this until one player gets 4 matching cards, for example 4 aces.

The winner then silently puts his finger on his nose.

The loser is the last player to put their finger on their nose.

<u>Regular forfeit;</u> Loser drinks a shot

<u>Interesting forfeit;</u> Loser drinks a shot and the winner gets to pick what shot it is.

Bonus Section 3
Inspiring quotes;

She had a head on her like:

A stuntman's knee,
A burnt welly*,
A slapped arse,
A bulldog licking piss off a nettle.

More Inspiration from the Motherland;

I wouldn't ride her into battle
She's no prize pony but I'd ride her around the house
The tide wouldn't take her out
Sweating like a horses fanny
About as welcome as a fart in a spacesuit
She'd breastfeed a kindergarten
An arse that moves like two pigs fighting under a blanket
An arse like two eggs in a hanky
He's as tight as a ducks arse
Any port in a storm (when times are tough with the opposite sex)

Chapter 4
In the Pub

The drink is flowing and the smell of banter is in the air so what better chance to get a good game going.

The on-location drinking game is typically the most expensive place to get involved, unless of course a sneaky shoulder or hip-flask is mothered* into the establishment. However, the price can always be justified by an electric atmosphere, attractive members of the opposite sex or the buzz of the big occasion.

Generally speaking, the more people that are around as any good drinking game progresses to its later stages the better. What better places than the pub or the nightclub to reenact Braveheart with your band of now invincible comrades?

Board games can also be a great addition to a day spent in the pub with some good forfeits added.

This chapter will give you some good ideas and quick games that can raise the buzz factor at any event.

Shnaggle Puss

A couple of old comrades used to go by the names Shnaggle*
Puss and Shnaggle Puff.

The rivalry progressed to the stage where they would whip
drinks off random bystanders leaving the unsuspecting
revellers to look down in horror at where their drink used to be
and find the following business card staring them in the face.

The actual business card is below.
Just try not to get caught...

Thank you and Kind Regards!!

Shnaggle R Puss Esq.

Other side of the bar
Yankme, Danglers
Galway,
Ireland
shnaggled@getyourselfapint.com

Ride Your Neighbour

Players: 🎩🎩🎩🎩+
Buzz Type: Deadly 🍺🍺🍺🍺
Equipment: Pitchers of beer

Gather a band of merry revellers together at the nearest bar with cheap pitchers you can find.

Buy a pitcher.

Each person then takes a turn drinking out of the pitcher, drinking as much or as little as they want and then passing the pitcher clockwise.

Key Rules:

When someone finishes the pitcher, the person to his right has to buy the next pitcher.

As you can see, the person who just passed you the pitcher is 'on the hook'.

The point and strategy of the game is to finish the pitcher if you can. If you don't finish the pitcher and the next guy you pass it on to does, you are caught buying the next one.

The inescapable result is that everyone ends up trying to pound a pitcher, and most won't finish it.

So, on top of getting hammered and likely puking, the unsuccessful pounder* has to waddle to the bar and buy the next pitcher.

This game can be played with pints as well but there is a much greater chance of contracting the herp* off a pint glass...

Beat the Barman

Players: +
Buzz Type: Deadly
Equipment: Pub, cash.

I don't know of anyone that's played this game to a finish.

You'll need your own barman (a quiet bar is usually best) and a ton of cash.

You order a drink and pay with a banknote that will require the barman to get you change.

You must have your drink finished by the time he returns with the change.

Order a new drink and repeat.

You win if the bar closes or the barman starts to cry.

You lose if you fall over or get turfed* out.

Lucky Dip

Players: 🎩🎩🎩+
Buzz Type: **Medium** 🍺🍺
Equipment: **Set of pre-written tasks, pints.**

There is a bit of preparation goes into this one.

You have to sit down with your friends and come up with a number of forfeits together, such as: kiss the waitress, offer to buy the dirtiest looking person in the pub a pint, insult someone's clothes and/or face, start a conga line etc.

Sit in a group with your friends, in a pub, club or other social setting where there are plenty of strangers around.

Everyone gets themselves a drink or three, then someone picks a task randomly from the pile.

If that person doesn't complete the task he/she has to chug a beer and has to pick another task.

If the person completes their task, everyone else has to chug a beer and that person gets to pick the next person to choose from the pile.

Use your imagination to come up with some freaky tasks but remember, it could be you!

Pub Golf

Players: +
Buzz Type: **Deadly** 🍺🍺🍺🍺
Equipment: **Money, 18 pubs in the area.**

You need to have 18 bars close together.

Galway, Belfast or Dublin are pretty good spots for this. There are plenty of suitable towns in the Americas for this one as well.

Each bar is a hole.

At each hole you drink a pint of beer (usually Guinness for this one). The number of drinks you take to finish the pint is your score for that hole. Score keeping might get a bit tricky after a few holes.

It is possible to play a 9 hole course but this game is usually reserved for windier* players.

Irish Coins

Players: 🎩🎩+
Buzz Type: Medium 🍺🍺
Equipment: Coin, cup, beer.

Start by filling a cup half full of beer.

Spin the quarter.

Drink the beer in the cup.

Fill the cup with more beer.

Grab the quarter before it stops spinning.

The next person repeats the above process.

If the quarter stops spinning before you stop it you must drink whatever you poured into the cup.

You're A Bollox*

Players: 🎩🎩🎩+
Buzz Type: High 🍺🍺🍺
Equipment: **Pub, balls the size of a Bengali Tiger*.**

This game starts with a race to see who can drink their pint fastest.

Whoever finishes last is then the 'messenger', the other people at the table are the 'winners'.

The 'winners' then tell the 'messenger' to go up and stand beside a random person in the bar for at least 60 seconds and the only words that they're allowed to say to the person is "You're a bollox!".

They are NOT ALLOWED to say why they are doing it, or apologize.

Other challenges can be designed to find the 'winner' and the 'messenger' but the forfeit has to be the same.

The most craic* ensues when the 'winners' send the 'messengers' to the same person in the pub over and over. Fun for all of the family.

Bonus Section 4
Karaoke

It's important that you remember some karaoke songs that will get you out of a sticky situation!

If you can't sing;

The Fields of Athenry

I Like Big Butts (Sir Mix a Lot)

I've Got Friends in Low Places (Garth Brooks)

Anything by Ringo Starr
(Octopuses Garden, Yellow Submarine)

Hurt (Johny Cash)

What a Wonderful World – Louis Armstrong (you need to put on your lowest, deepest blues voice, like you're gargling a turnip)

The Way I Are (Timbaland)

Ice Ice Baby (Vanilla Ice)

If you can sing a few bars;

Whisky in the Jar (Thin Lizzy)

Walking in Memphis (Marc Cohn)

Superfreak (Rick James)

Somebodies Watching Me (Mysto & Pizzi - Geico)

Total Eclipse of the Heart (Dan Band)

Chapter 5
After Party

So the jager bombs are down the hatch, the beer jackets are on and nobody even flinches about the 2 mile walk back, in Baltic conditions, to the free house for some after hour hijinks. This is the part of the night that can separate the tea bags from the tea baggers, the Michael Knights from the lonely nights.

There is the potential for more alcohol to be consumed during the after party, than at any other stage of the night. This is generally because people are already shteamed* and the cheap liquor that used to taste like diesel now tastes like Mothers milk*. Quite simply, this is survival of the fittest on the grandest stage.

But with great risk also comes great reward. Some of the greatest treasures can be uncovered at the after party. Games can come to life and inhibitions tend to be left at the door. Even the vegan in the corner wants to get involved in a game of bobbing for chops! You can find and lose a potential partner 10 times over at a good after party, so in essence all is yet to play for, even though the novices are already tucked up under the covers.

Hide And Drink

Players: 🎩🎩🎩+
Buzz Type: **Medium** 🍺🍺
Equipment: **Somewhere to hide, beer.**

Let me introduce this one by saying you have to be beyond belted*
drunk to play this one.

It's good old traditional 'Hide and Seek' with a twist.

Everyone stumbles off and tries to find a hiding place as the seeker
counts to twenty.

If the seeker finds you in the first thirty seconds you have to chug the
drink that you are hiding with.

Wait until you are nose deep, snorkeling in the back of the couch trying
to hide and then tell me if it still sounds easy.

Might take some convincing to get the game going but believe me it's
worth it.

Night at the Races

Players: 🎩🎩+
Buzz Type: **High** 🍺🍺🍺
Equipment: **Deck of cards and drink of choice.**

"A racehorse is the only animal that can take thousands of people for a ride at the same time" – anonymous.

First take all the kings and queens out of the deck and line them up in a straight line, making the horse track.

Then take the aces (horses) out and line them next to the first king or Queen, so they make an 'L' shape.

Then everyone bets on which horse (ace) they think will win the race. Give each ace a horses name for a more personal touch.

Then take the deck and turn the top card over.

Depending on the suit of the card turned, the horse 'ace' of that suit then moves along the track, of kings and queens, one spot.

Continue turning cards until the first horse crosses the finish line.

You can gamble whatever you want on the race.

A favorite forfeit is for the winner to saddle up the loser and ride him/her around the house.

More than one person can bet on the same horse. If two people bet on the same horse they each get to give out the number of drinks agreed at the start.

Some good horse names for you:

- Cunning Stunt.

- Hoof Hearted – say this a few times fast hur hur.

- Panty Raid.

- Seadonkey.

- Cherry Pop.

- Peg-leg.

- Spider-pig.

Pikey* Poker

Players: 🎩🎩🎩+
Buzz Type: **Medium** 🍺🍺
Equipment: **Deck of cards, beer.**

A full deck of cards is placed in the center of the table.

Each player draws one card and without looking at it places it face out on their forehead (so everyone but them sees it).

One by one each player, running clockwise from the dealer, in turn folds or stays.

The player who stays with the lowest card drinks for as many seconds as the number on the winners card.

For example: If the first player has a 4 and everyone else folds but the last player, and he has a 9, the first player takes 9 drinks.

If only one person stays in and everyone else folds then everyone drinks the amount of drinks on the winner's card.

Face cards are 10 points. Aces are 15.

If your stupid enough to stay when someone has an ace then you deserve it.

If you cheat by sneaking a peek at your card and get caught, well that's 20 drinks, because you DESERVE IT.

Last man standing wins!!!

Disarm The Bomb

Players: +
Buzz Type: Deadly 🍺🍺🍺🍺
Equipment: 4 cans or bottles of any size and tape.

You firstly need to tape four beers together, in a cube shape.

Then, you choose the escape artist whose job it will be to diffuse the bomb.

You tape his/her hand to one of the four beers, and give them ten minutes to diffuse the bomb.

The bomb can only be defused by drinking all of the beer.

If the person cannot diffuse the bomb, either by not drinking fast enough or puking or whatnot, all those watching must dump the remains of their beer on the person's head.

Harsh but fair!

Wait until you see how much of the beer from the bomb ends up on the artists head whether they win, lose or draw.

This game can also be used as a forfeit.

Twenty One

Players: 🎩🎩🎩+
Buzz Type: High 🍺🍺🍺
Equipment: Drink.

You would want a few bevvies in the system before you start playing this one.

All players sit around in a circle or around a table.

The idea is simple, you count around the group one player at a time, from one to twenty one, with each person calling one number at a time.

Except, the number 13 is represented by a 'farting sound' and not saying 13, any multiple of 3 is replaced with 'tree' and multiples of 5 are replaced with 'Bollox'.

If the player says the number or gets the action wrong, he or she must drink the forfeit and then substitute any other number not already assigned, between 1 and 21, with an action for that number.

By the time all the numbers have actions assigned to them, you'll be doing well to get to 21.

Blow Pong

Players: 🎩🎩🎩🎩+
Buzz Type: Medium 🍺🍺
Equipment: Table, ping pong ball, beer.

Each player gets their own beer.

Everyone has to get down on their knees or bend down low enough so they can easily blow the ping pong ball around the table.

You can either do this in teams or every man for himself defending a side of the table.

It must be said, a square table is the fairest for this game but it doesn't really matter.

The object is to blow the ball off the table on any your opponent's sides.

You can not use your hands or block the pong with anything.

You can only use your own hot, windy air.

Start the ball in the middle of the table, and when someone says "GO" you all start blowing.

When the ball rolls off the table, the player who's side it went off has to chug a beer.

People will be fainting all over the show

Kinky coins

Players: 🎩🎩🎩🎩+
Buzz Type: Medium 🍺🍺
Equipment: Pint of beer for each player, 1 coin and some randy players.

Each player sits in a circle with their mug of beer in front of them.

Players take turns in any pre-determined order.

One player will try to bounce a quarter into another's cup.

The player can pick anyone's cup to try they want.

If the player gets the quarter into his victim's cup, that person must 'talk dirty' to him/her (eg: 'I love you long time' etc) for 30 seconds.

If either party hesitates at any stage during the 30 seconds, they must chug their beer.

If the dirty talker gets through the 30 seconds without laughing or hesitating, the recipient of the roasting has to chug their beer.

This is a good game
to play to feel out a
potential ride!

Bonus Section 5
Seasonal Events

Christmas

12 pubs of Christmas

This is an annual event when friends are back for the holidays from afar and meet up for a session. The night consists of one drink in each of 12 separate pubs around the town.

Santacon

This is a great event you can look up in your hometown. Hundreds and thousands of people gather in different cities around the world, dress up in Christmas outfits and go on a session for the day. This is a great event that everyone should get involved in at least once.

You can find more information by searching for Santacon online.

Summer

Beer Olympics

You can host your own beer Olympics by using games from this book or other games you make up yourself. Separate people into teams (Countries) or individuals and let the games begin!

Bike Ride

Same principal as 12 pubs of Christmas above except you cycle from bar to bar with a group of people. Great fun but stay off the road.

Glossary

Arse – Bottom.
Balls the size of a Bengali Tiger – Large testicles.
Banter – Having a good laugh.
Belted – Drunk.
Belter – Great.
Blocked – Drunk.
Bollix – Testes.
Bollox – see 'Bollix'.
Bowsy – Messer or someone who is always causing trouble.
Craic – Having a laugh, also 'are you having the craic?'.
Dirty Fry – Irish breakfast of sausage, beans, fried eggs & black pudding.
Dry Shite – Miserable.
Flamin' Drunk – Extremely drunk.
Grease the Pony – Having a few drinks to get you in the mood.
Hammered – Drunk.
Mothered – Hidden or sneaked.
Mothers Milk – Tastes great.
Peg Legged – Clumsy or awkward.
Pikey – see the movie 'Snatch' for reference.
Piss-head – Drunk.
Pound – Downing a drink in one.
Prick – General insult.
Shite – Not great.
Shnaggled – see 'Mothered'.
Shteamed – Hammered drunk.
Skanks – Tricks.
Smart Arse – Someone who is a bit of a know it all.
Snoz – Nose.
Snotzer – Someone with a defined nose.
Taking the Mick – Making fun of something/someone.
The Herp – Herpes/Mono.
Turfed – Thrown or given out to.
Welly – Wellington boot or rain boot.
Windy – Not as determined or involved.

Feckin Flys!

An Englishman, a Scot, and the Beef walked into a pub. Each orderd a pint of beer. Then a fly landed in each one's beer.

The Englishman, turning slightly green, pushed his beer away and asked for another one.

The Scot took the fly out, shrugged, and drank his beer.

The Beef pinched the fly between his fingers and yelled

"SPIT IT OUT YA PRICK!" "SPIT IT OUT!"